Mostly
SANTA BARBARA

Lynn Richardson

Tea House restaurant—see Fig. 59.

Mostly

SANTA BARBARA

A collection of pen-and-ink drawings
created in and around Santa Barbara
over a thirty-year time span
from Ventura, Carpinteria, Summerland,
Montecito, Goleta & the Santa Ynez Valley
to San Francisco

PEN-AND-INK DRAWINGS
BY
LYNN RICHARDSON

FITHIAN PRESS / SANTA BARBARA / 1998

Copyright ©1998 Lynn W. Richardson
All rights reserved
Printed in the United States of America
Published by Fithian Press
A division of Daniel and Daniel, Publishers, Inc.
Post Office Box 1525
Santa Barbara, CA 93102

Book design: Lynn Richardson
Production: Tom Moore
Editor: David Dahl

ISBN #1-56474-301-2

Figure 1: Valentine bunnies, advertisement.

This book is dedicated to the memory
of my parents, Loys and Frank,
and to my peerless husband,
Armin Müller.

Figure 2: Reading cats, from a YES Store advertisement.

CONTENTS

	Figure Numbers
Buildings & Habitats	4-26
Businesses, Services & Offices	27-81
Interiors	82-98
Gardens, Plants & Trees	99-111
Beach & Shore	112-119
Animals	120-158
Holidays	159-202
Maps	203-209
Objects & Borders	210-228

Introduction

From my early childhood, drawing and coloring gave me, along with a creative outlet, my balance and drive, a focus. I went to all the after-school craft classes and took all the art classes I possibly could in junior high and high school. In college, at San Jose State, I studied art education and received a B.A. and a teaching credential in 1965. I subsequently taught high school for two years and then decided to go out on my own and take my chances as an artist, where my heart was. After college I'd taken up drawing in earnest, determined to improve my skills. As my teachers had advised, I carried my pen and sketchbook everywhere I went. Quitting that job was my first real test as an artist, but I was determined.

Looking back at those earliest years of my career I'm proudest of the fact that through the combination of inner drive, the honing of my skills, and economic necessity I was able to meet the challenges that came with finding commercial art jobs, dealing with clients, and producing successful work, both in terms of pleasing clients, and my own eye. I forced myself to sit down on public streets, in all types of neighborhoods, on my little folding camp stool, under my straw hat, with minimal tools to capture a reasonable likeness of a house, a tree, or an office building, in spite of wind, rain, hot sun, birds overhead (if you know what I mean) and the comments, good and bad, of passersby. This is how I worked for many years, on location, without using photographs, other reference materials (like books on trees, for instance), or copy machines.

My first commercial job came through artist Ted Villa–the logo for Cafe Del Sol, which they still use. My abilities for these early jobs were enriched by taking classes in printmaking (including etching) at Santa Barbara's Adult Education with Ron Robertson and Gary Chafe. During these years, in the late sixties and early seventies, my "artistic life" was also enhanced through acquaintances with local craftspeople such as Armin Müller and Chafe, who started the YES Store tradition back in 1969. Over the following fifteen years or so, I participated in the Sunday art shows at the beach with another artist, Alice Shaw, in the Old Mission 4th of July art shows, and in the Renaissance Pleasure Faires. Most of my commercial jobs came through meeting people at these events or via word-of-mouth through other friends and acquaintances.

The literally largest job I've ever done was in 1989, when I was asked by designer Sandra Canada if I thought I could repaint the two-story tall Santa Claus at Santa Claus Lane near Carpinteria. I immediately said, "Not a chance!" But then, the more I thought about it, the more I became tempted by the idea of painting something so huge, and such a landmark–I changed my mind and did it. Although finally a satisfying experience, it was a frightening ordeal, in many ways, as you might imagine.

I'm often asked by someone looking at one of my detailed drawings, "How long did it take to do that?" Drawings of the interiors of houses where I've lived, the bathroom (fig. 84), kitchens (figs. 83 and 85), or other rooms (fig. 92) are approximately twice the size reproduced here and took between ten and fifteen hours to do. I think the largest pen-and-ink drawing I've ever done was of Victoria Court (fig. 207). It was done at the site and is about twenty inches square. The Santa Barbara Street scene (fig. 26) and Santa Claus Lane (fig. 27) are each about twenty-eight inches long. I should say at this point that I looked over about one thousand of my drawings in order to make the selections for this book.

Unfortunately, I wasn't savvy enough in the sixties to make copies of the work I did at that time, so many of those don't appear here. Tom Moore and Armin helped me select the two hundred and thirty or so drawings that made the "final cut."

Years and years of bending over a drawing board or drafting table, gardening, and building our house from the ground up have taken a toll on me physically. Consequently, I'm no longer soliciting new clients, but continue to work with some with whom I've had a wonderful working relationship for many years. Also, I've begun exploring an entirely new genre–small-scale sculptures…but that's grist for the next book. With this change in my artistic focus, and as I've grown older, I feel compelled to pull my life's work together, see what it all looks like in one place, clean out old files, organize, put stuff in order, complete the circle that began in grammar school art classes so long ago. This book accomplishes much of the above for me, pulling many threads of my journey together into a coherent whole. Many drawings are like pages from a diary of my life and times. Some of these drawings will also stir the memories of other Santa Barbarans, as they depict places, businesses, no longer in existence, or that have changed location.

And that's a key word here–*change*. People and places have changed. Some businesses moved, one burned down, and another, a restaurant in Hawaii, was destroyed by hurricane Ewa! Friendships have formed. Some became marriages. Husbands, wives and friends, surprised each other with gifts of drawings (fig. 23). Some clients have moved away. Some, sadly, have died. About two weeks before our friend Tom Fernandes died, he asked me to draw his house as a gift to his family. That was a tough assignment, which I hurried to complete in time for him to see it.

I've enjoyed a good life in Santa Barbara. Fortune has smiled on me–I have been one of the lucky ones, able to be what I always wanted to be, an artist. I present these images of a lifetime for your enjoyment.

Mostly
SANTA BARBARA

Figure 3: Collection of neighborhood mailboxes, Coyote Road.

BUILDINGS & HABITATS

Homes • Trailers • Teepee • Garages & Neighborhoods

Figure 4: Montecito home, drawn for a real estate brochure.

Figure 5: This illustration of Montecito was drawn to promote the annual "Montecito Beautification Day" celebration and was a gift to my community.

MONTECITO

Figure 6: Tiny Montecito cottage, drawn for our musician friend Hank.

Figure 7: Our friend Billy's garage and former woodworking shop.

Figure 8: Two old friends of ours (building contractors) lived "outdoors" like we did, and they wanted to preserve the scene in pen and ink before moving into the homes they were building in Carpinteria. Two intricate drawings were traded for framing my studio (see Figure 22).

Figure 9: Rickey's house, Clearview Road.

CLEARVIEW RD.

Figure 10: I traded this drawing of Erin & John's house for two of her wonderful large hand-tinted photographs.

Figure 11: Drawing of our homestead in Sycamore Canyon during the three and a half years we lived in the garage, doing dishes at the bath house, outdoors, while we built our house with our own hands.

Figure 12: One of my favorite homes with lots of character on Santa Barbara Street.

Figure 13: I sat on top of Michael's van all day to draw this shingled home on Salsipuedes Street.

Figure 14: A nice window.

Figure 15: The house where Armin lived and had his pottery studio, in the early days, on Carrillo Street.

Figure 16: Imaginary Victorian house.

Figure 17: Mellifont Street home, commissioned as a gift to the owner from friends.

Figure 18: San Francisco Victorian.

Figure 19: Imaginary Victorian home.

Figure 20: Drawing of a house on Brinkerhoff Avenue, which was used as a business card by the owner.

Figure 21: Teepee, rubber stamp design.

Figure 22: This was the second drawing traded for the labor and expertise to frame my studio. See Fig. 8.

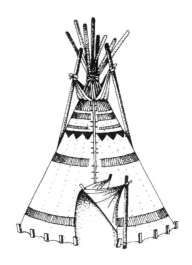

Figure 23: My client commissioned this drawing of their new house in Hope Ranch as a surprise gift to his wife.

Figure 24: Kitty and Steve's house at El Rancho Hacienda, off Mountain Drive.

Figure 25: Nice Spanish-style home bordering Plaza Bonita.

Figure 26: Most of the 500 block of Santa Barbara Street, with my perfect 30-year-old Volkswagen parked in front.

See Figure 74: Joe's Cafe.

BUSINESSES, SERVICES & OFFICES

Storefronts • Offices (Doctors, Hospitals, Dentists, Veterinarians) • Advertisements & Announcements • Banks • Airport • Fire Station Markets • Hotels • Galleries & Theatre

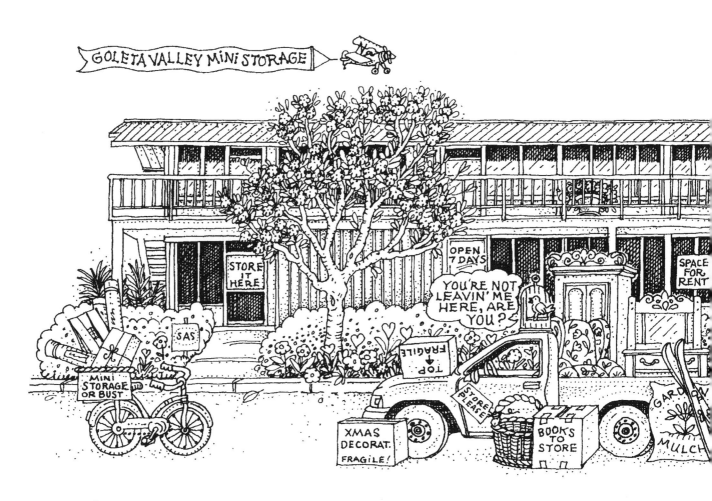

Figure 27: After I was commissioned to redesign and paint the old Santa Claus and his chimney at Santa Claus Lane, the owners commissioned this drawing of all the shops and eateries for the menu at the Reindeer Room.

Figure 28: Drawing used for advertisements for Goleta Valley Mini-Storage.

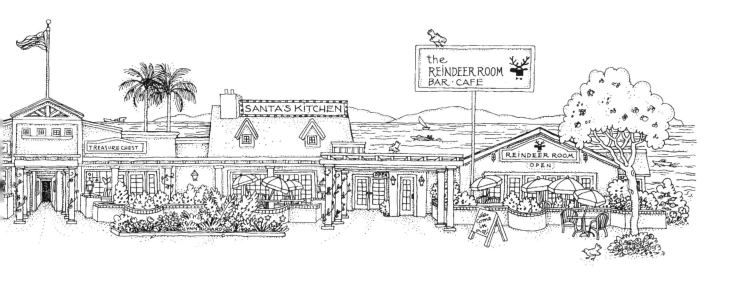

Figure 29: Window display for El Paseo Sweet Shop.

Figure 30: The Tennis Shop, Montecito.

Figure 31: My perception of the variety of people who are clients of my accountant, David Peri.

Figure 32: Display at W.A. King, for Women.

Figure 33: Interior of W.A. King, for Men, drawn on site.

W.A. King company

Figure 34: Interior of Hen's Nest restaurant on Santa Barbara Street, drawn while sitting on a stool next to the toaster.

Figure 35: Interior of W.A. King Co., for Men, Solvang.

Figure 36: Drawing of Haley Street fire station, No. 2, a gift for Mike Jacobs on his retirement.

Figure 37: W.A. King Company, for Men, Figueroa Street at La Arcada Court.

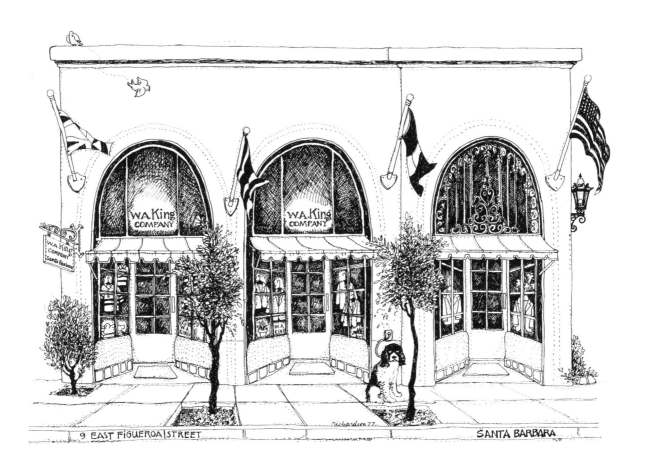

Figure 38: Building drawn for real estate brochure, Victoria and Chapala Street.

Figure 39: Captain Quick's Seafood Cafe, in Victoria Court.

Figure 40: Stampa Barbara, A Rubberstamp Paradise, as it was in El Paseo.

Figure 41: Easu's Coffee Shop, the best breakfast in town. The drawing was a gift from me to Tom Esau, the original owner. He was a nice guy.

Figure 42: The Darkroom Workshop on Santa Barbara Street was a gift from a friend of the owner. I was drawing it when an enormous R.V. pulled into the parking space in front. I had to pack up and return the next day.

Figure 43: Galeria Del Mar, on the wharf.

Figure 44: The best tree and landscape guy in town and our good friend. Duke loves his own trees and the view from our neighborhood.

Figure 45: Small World, a special store for children.

Figure 46: Shopping at Victoria Court.

Figure 47: Clients at Bodyfirm (the artist is third from the left).

Figure 48: Hearts Delight, storefront, in Carpinteria.

Figure 49: The Big Yellow House, Summerland.

Figure 50: St. Francis professional buildings, surgical wing, hospital, the Riviera Building, Alta Riviera Building & Micheltorena Medical Plaza.

Figure 51: Stampa Barbara, A Rubberstamp Paradise, Paseo Nuevo.

Figure 52: Office of my wonderful dentist, Dr. Alan P. Williams, Alamar Professional Building.

Figure 53: The La Arcada Court clock, State Street.

Figure 54: Office of Dr. Claude Yeoman, D.D.S, Arrellaga Street.

Figure 55: Mission Santa Barbara.

Figure 56: The Cat Clinic, Mission Street. The drawing was given to the veterinarian by her friends.

Figure 57: Barry's nice old brick office building on State Street, which later burned to the ground.

Figure 58: Logo for La Arcada Court.

Figure 59: The Tea House restaurant on Canon Perdido Street, where I supplemented my artist's income waitressing in the early seventies.

Figure 60: Usually called the Faulding Hotel, for a brief time this building was the Old Town Inn.

Figure 61: Mr. Kim's Chinese-American grocery on Canon Perdido Street.

Figure 62: Window display at Mr. Kim's Chinese-American grocery.

Figure 63: Advertisement for Run Ragged, a service that takes care of all your personal needs.

Figure 64: Advertisement for Gillio's Rare Coins and Fine Jewelry on State Street.

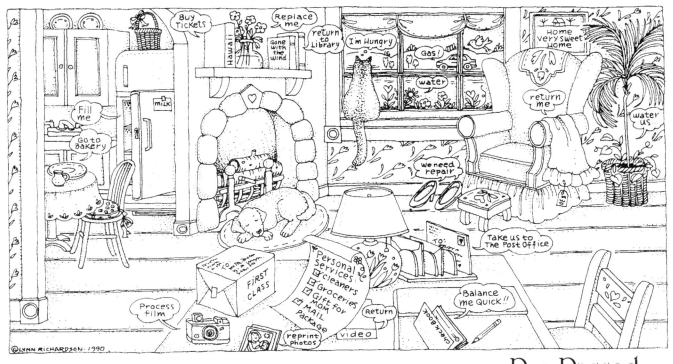

Run Ragged
A Personal Service

Figure 65: Advertisement for Aeroplane Advertising Co., Santa Ynez Valley.

Figure 66: Advertisement for City Commerce Bank, State Street at La Cumbre. I was impressed that Don Dancer, the art director, said the bank wanted something this fun.

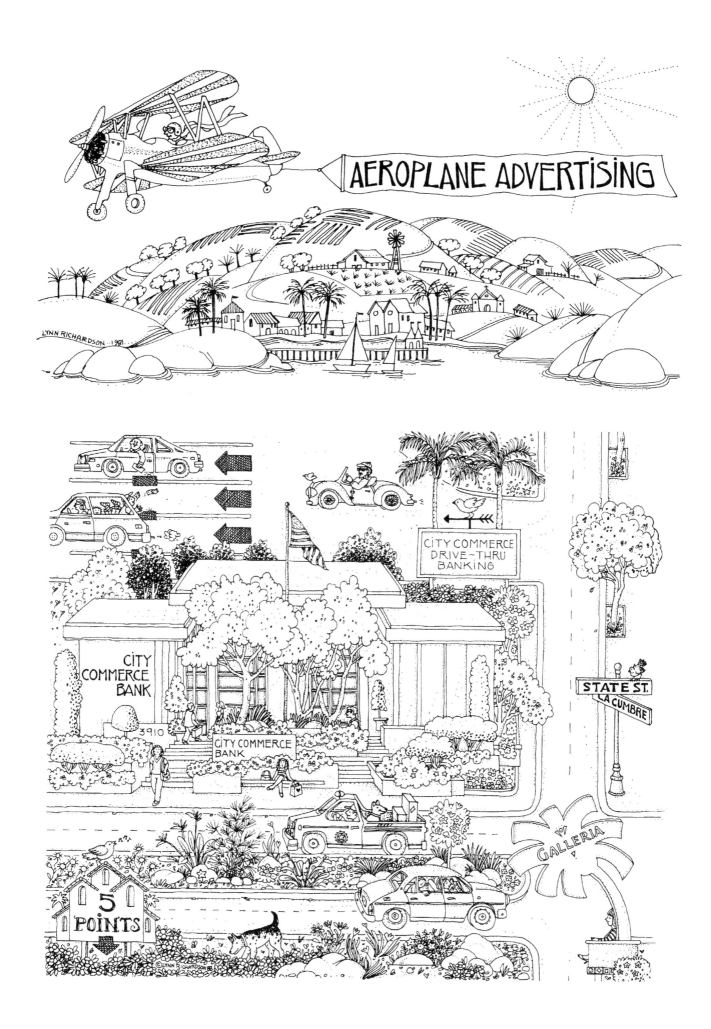

Figure 67: Stampa Barbara, A Rubberstamp Paradise, in El Paseo. This was Gary Dorothy's first storefront. The Grand Canyon of rubber stamps, I used to call it. It was a tightly packed little shop.

Figure 68: L. Scott & Co., Brinkerhoff Avenue.

Figure 69: Office for rent, Chapala Street.

Figure 70: Elizabeth Fortner's first gallery, State Street.

Figure 71: The La Concepción Animal Hospital of Dr. James Bond, D.V.M.

Figure 72: Window and friends at the Milpas St. pet store.

Figure 73: La Paloma Cafe, Anacapa Street.

Figure 74: Joe's Cafe. The best cafe. The drawing was done for owner Nancy Peery as a thank you from me. It was one of the most interesting places to draw on site, due in part to a very persistent gentlemen desiring a date for lunch.

Figure 75: Headline banner for the *Blue Sky News*, an informative newspaper published by the Santa Barbara Airport.

Figure 76: A nice lady waiting to board the plane.

Figure 77: Departing passengers. For *Blue Sky News*.

Figure 78: Poster advertising the third annual Airport Day.

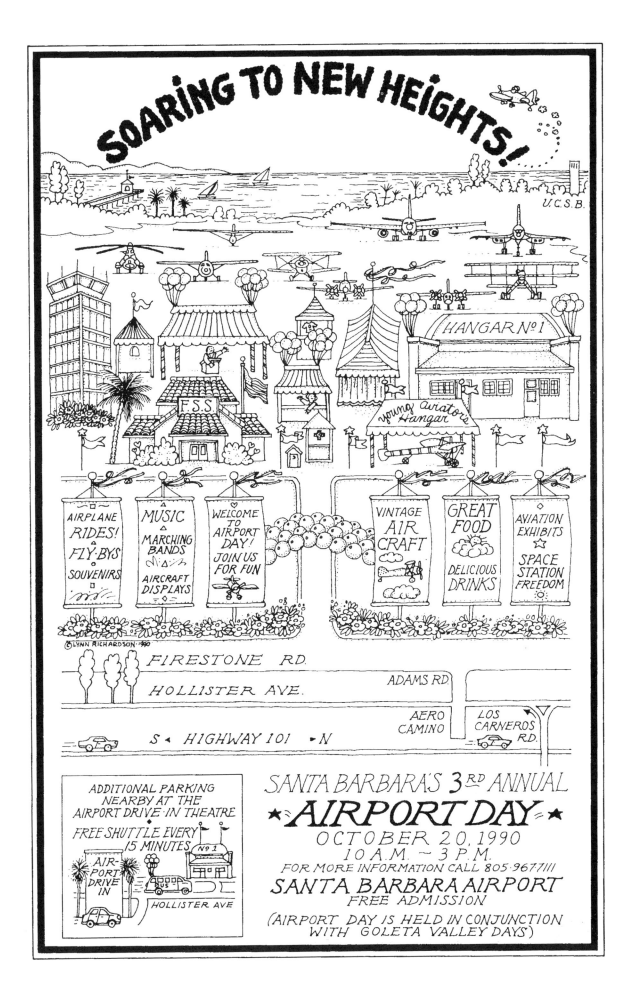

Figure 79: Poster to wish Al Wiengand a happy birthday and to advertise a fundraiser for the Community Environmental Council.

Figure 80: The Lobero Theatre.

Figure 81: Mountain Drive kitchen, home of the Neelys.

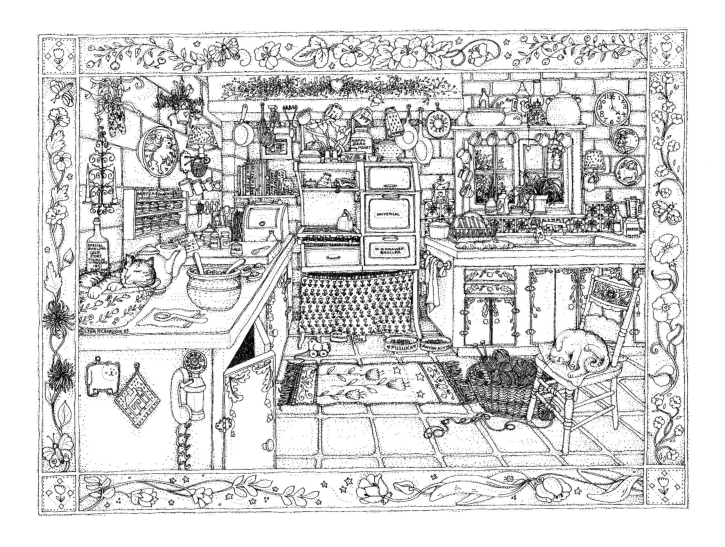

INTERIORS
Kitchens • Bedrooms & Sitting Rooms
Bathrooms • Shops & Stores

Figure 82: Annette's sewing room, on the porch of her home on Puesta del Sol.

Figure 83: My wonderful tiny kitchen at Hidden Hollow on Grand Avenue, Apartment F. Hidden Hollow was a magical place for six years when I first came to Santa Barbara. The kitchen was really a small square, but I couldn't figure our how to draw it that way.

Figure 84: My little tiny square bathroom at Hidden Hollow, with all my stuff on display.

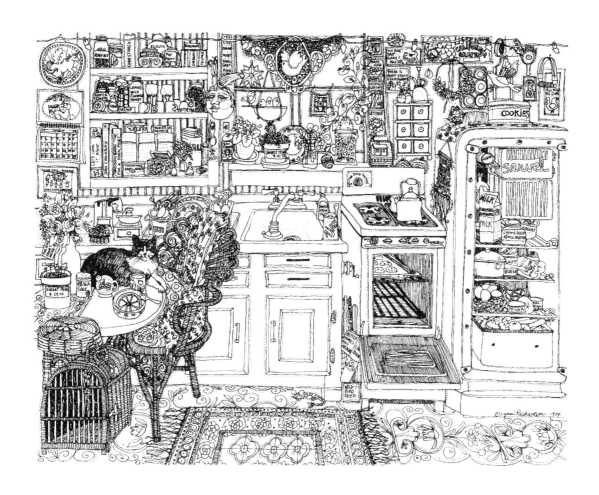

Figure 85: The kitchen on Carrillo Street, after I moved in and started trapping the mice, in 1975. There were a lot of wild cats.

Figure 86: Imaginary kitchen.

Figure 87: Brass bed for bed & breakfast brochure.

Figure 88: The Carrillo Street stove, relocated to the garage on the mountain where we cooked on it before moving it (again) to the completed house.

Figure 89: Also part of our garage/kitchen.

Figure 90: Oak bed for a brochure.

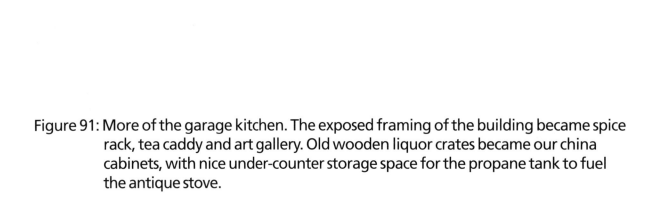

Figure 91: More of the garage kitchen. The exposed framing of the building became spice rack, tea caddy and art gallery. Old wooden liquor crates became our china cabinets, with nice under-counter storage space for the propane tank to fuel the antique stove.

Figure 92: My room on Carrillo Street with David Carlin's dog Bullfrog and some of our cats.

Figure 93: Bedroom. I can't remember whose, for sure.

Figure 94: Sherry's kitchen on Puesta del Sol.

Figure 95: Imaginary bathroom.

Figure 96: The everything-came-from-the-1902-Sears-Roebuck-Catalog bathroom.

Figure 97: Imaginary bedroom.

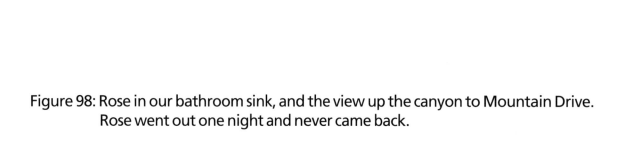

Figure 98: Rose in our bathroom sink, and the view up the canyon to Mountain Drive. Rose went out one night and never came back.

Figure 99: Whirligig in our vegetable garden.

GARDENS
Gardens • Plants & Trees

Figure 100: The Community Environmental Council's community garden on the east side of town.

Figure 101: Anastasia's garden. This drawing was a gift from her husband. So was the tiny little alligator, who grew up, got loose in the garden and was very tricky to catch for the ride to the Griffith Park Zoo.

Figure 102: Vegetables and fruits, used for rubber stamp design.

Figure 103: Gift basket from the Village Fair shop.

Figure 104: Agapanthus.

Figure 105: Porch from bed & breakfast brochure.

Figure 106: California poppies.

Figure 107: My favorite swap-meet purchase, a cracked pitcher made to look like a cottage, with a cup made by my husband.

Figure 108: Oak tree, stationery design.

Figure 109: Saguaro cactus, stationery design.

Figure 110: Ant, rubber stamp design.

Figure 111: Garden tools & watering can, rubber stamp design.

Figure 112: Menu design, Whaler's Cove restaurant, Poipu Beach, Kauai.
The restaurant was smashed flat by big waves during hurricane Ewa.

BEACH & SHORE

Figure 113: The Sunday arts & crafts show at the beach, in which I participated for about seven years.

Figure 114: Dog-powered skating at the beach.

Figure 115: Windsurfing at Santa Barbara.

Figure 116: The Havana, drawn on site, two times, for the live-aboard family. The first time was a failure after I included the mast of a neighboring vessel.

Figure 117: Whale, for a sign.

Figure 118: Tugboat Julie, a gift from the owner's good friend.

Figure 119: Shells for Tower's Interiors logo.

See Figure 136: Cat in a bag.

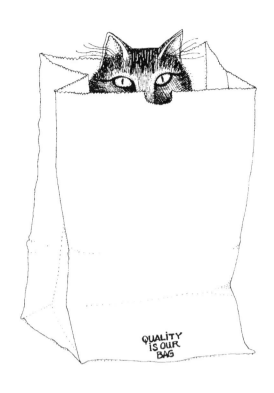

ANIMALS
Cats • Dogs • Birds • Rabbits
Ducks • Geese • Goats & Others

Figure 120: Mom cat and kittens for Mother's Day advertisement.

Figure 121: This drawing celebrated the surprise appearance of a California black bear at Ed Schertz' house above Mountain Drive.

Figure 122: Roller polar, drawn for Lions, Tigers & Bears, Oh My, La Cumbre Plaza.

Figure 123: Easter drawing for an advertisement.

Figure 124: Mugs Freeman, of Lake Oswego, Oregon, a very cool cat.

Figure 125: Kitty dreams of flying, a drawing for a six-foot-long, hanging, two-sided, painted masonite piece for the 1985 Santa Barbara Art Museum "Artwalk."

Figure 126: Unicorn for Lions, Tigers & Bears, Oh My.

Figure 127: Bunny and flowers.

Figure 128: Bunnies.

Figure 129: Geese.

Figure 130: Goats.

Figure 131: Basket of kittens, rubber stamp design.

Figure 132: Love kitten, rubber stamp design.

Figure 133: Travel advertisement.

Figure 134: This Happy Bear Honey jar label was wonderful in full New Mexico color.

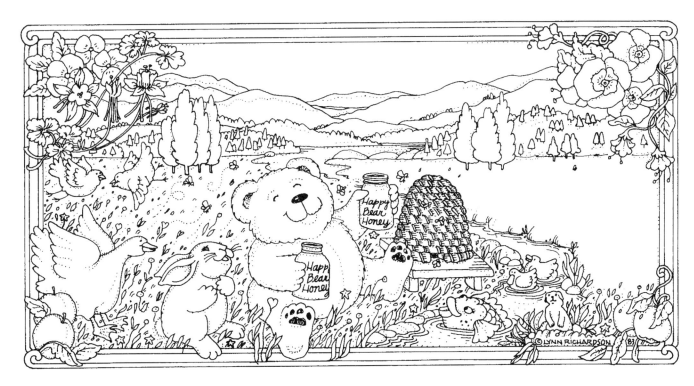

Figure 135: Hungry cat, rubber stamp design.

Figure 136: Cat in a bag, one of my best sellers in rubber stamp and postcard designs.

Figure 137: Puppet show, for Sandcastle Construction Company children's store.

Figure 138: Garden cats, drawing for a two-foot by six-foot, two-sided, painted masonite piece, for Santa Barbara Art Museum "Artwalk," 1986.

Figure 139: Radio cat, post card design.

Figure 140: Piano cat, rubber stamp design.

Figure 141: Rat on toast for dinner. Drawn from an old stereroscopic photograph of a real cat at a table with a stuffed (or dead) rat on a piece of toast.

Figure 142: Potluck cats, from a party invitation.

Figure 143: Advertisement to promote the Lobero Theatre.

Figure 144: Yard full of geese.

Figure 145: Easter chick for rubber stamp design.

Figure 146: Flying bear, for Small World, A Special Store for Children.

Figure 147: Party boys.

Figure 148: Animal faces, rubber stamp designs.

Figure 149: California quail, for a rubber stamp design.

Figure 150: Our Polish rooster, Phil Diller, whom Alex King liked to feature in ads used by W.A. King Co., for Men.

Figure 151: Shore birds, rubber stamp design.

Figure 152: Hand-carved wood block print design, created pro bono for proposed salmon fishery.

Figure 153: Cormorant, for rubber stamp design.

Figure 154: Hawk nesting in the side of an older building at the airport.

Figure 155: Butterfly.

Figure 156: From a newspaper article featuring Star the Samoyed.

Figure 157: Armadillo, for a stationery design.

Figure 158: Pet cemetery at the San Francisco Presidio.

Figure 159: Flying Happy New Year cat, our Christmas card, 1983.

HOLIDAYS

Figure 160: Santa Claus. my design for the renovation of the aging Santa Claus and chimney at Santa Claus Lane, 1989. Now he wears "real" gold-rimmed glasses, with real lenses, and he's much friendlier.

Figure 161: Christmas border for Small World, enclosing Christmas artwork for Victoria Court, and featuring my Halley's Comet cat from one of our own Christmas cards.

Figure 162: Advertisement for the YES Store.

Figure 163: YES Store, 1207 State Street, 1980.

Figure 164: YES Store, 1236 State Street, 1978.

Figure 165: Storefront, for the Village Fair Christmas card, 1988.

Figure 166: The night before Christmas, from the 1983 Village Fair Christmas card.

Figure 167: Christmas border, featuring crafts shown at the yearly YES Store, with a lady bear skating along with her wagon full of good things.

Figure 168: Christmas at Small World, Ventura.

Figure 169: Advertisement for Oshkosh jeans and merriment.

Figure 170: Holiday doorway, rubber stamp design.

Figure 171: Cookies for the holidays, rubber stamp design.

Figures 172-177 were all holiday rubber stamps, except for the Christmas tree for Small World. I probably drew 200 designs just for Stampa Barbara.

Figure 178: YES Store, 1983, 35 W. Canon Perdido.

Figure 179: More things for sale at the YES Store.

Figure 180: YES Store, 1987, 26 W. Anapamu Street.

Figure 181: Christmas card, our front yard, on Carrillo Street.

Figure 182: Christmas card, our back yard, on Carrillo Street.

Figure 183: Christmas card, our living room, on Carrillo Street.

Figure 184: Christmas card, our kitchen, on Carrillo Street.

Figure 185: Our front porch in Sycamore Canyon, at Christmastime, before we remodeled it.

Figure 186: Our Christmas card, 1978.

Figure 187: Valentine bunnies.

Figure 188: The Village Fair Christmas, Christmas card.

Figure 189: Christmas at P.S. Limited, La Arcada Court. My clients like to feature their beloved pets every year on their Christmas cards.

Figure 190: Mission Santa Barbara at Christmas.

Figure 191: The annual holiday boat parade in Santa Barbara Harbor.

Figure 192: Christmas with your dear ones around you.

Figure 193: P.S. Limited, making changes...scheduled to open after Christmas.

Figure 194: Christmas greetings from the Santa Ynez Valley.

Figure 195: Christmas in Santa Barbara. Can you find the Tea House and my house?

Figure 196: Welcome Katie's new friend, Sarah, for Christmas.

Figure 197: Christmas at La Arcada.

Figure 198: Home for the holidays.

Figure 199: Christmas preparations.

Figure 200: Farewell to Dillon, who ascended to heaven in 1996.

Figure 201 & 202: Angels, rubber stamp designs.

Figure 203: Map to antique shops on Brinkerhoff Avenue, completed on site in the early seventies. This was a fabulous commission, thanks to Wanda and Robert Livernois, and it led to many other jobs.

MAPS

Figure 204: Airplane for an article in the airport's *Blue Sky News.*

Figure 205: Map to guide visitors during the Airport Day celebration.

Figure 206: Map to find La Arcada Court.

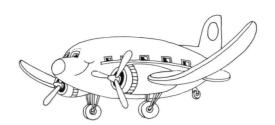

Figure 207: This map of Victoria Court was completed on site and was one of my most popular pieces; it led to more commissions of this kind.

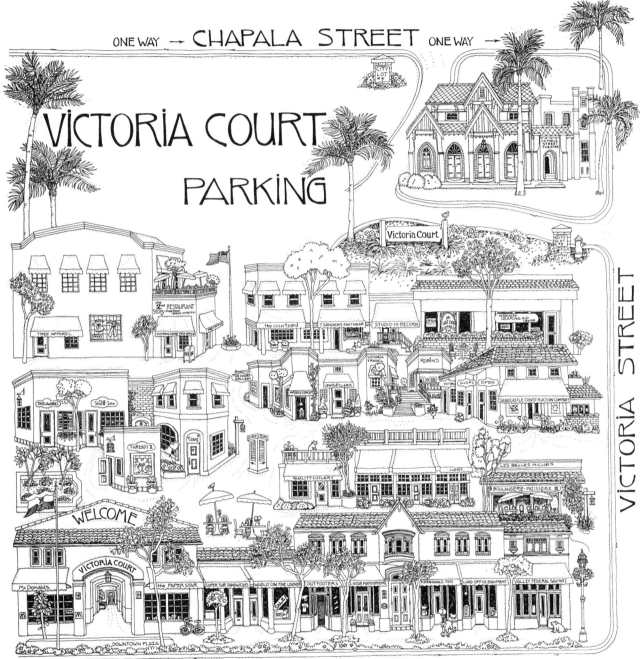

Figure 208: Another favorite map, La Arcada Court, also done on site, was a big challenge to arrange all the businesses in a front-facing way.

STATE STREET
La Arcada Court

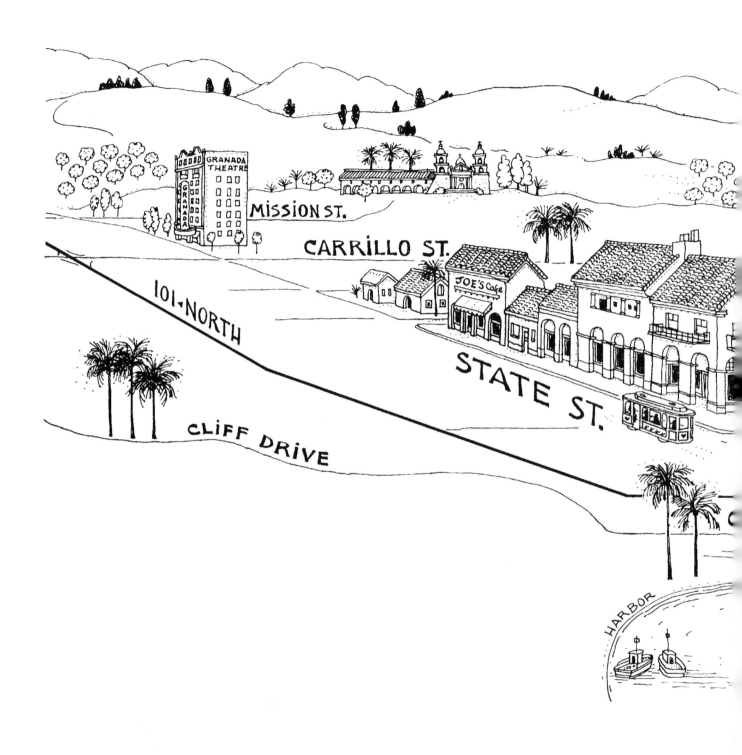

Figure 209: For a brief time the old Faulding Hotel was renamed the Old Town Inn, and this map was part of a promotional brochure. Now, the Faulding Hotel is back.

Figure 210: Ready to knit, rubber stamp design.

OBJECTS & BORDERS
Things For Sale
For Children
For Fun

Figure 211: The Lobero Theatre kiosk was used in a promotional brochure.

Figure 212: Christmas border.

Figure 213: Border with sewing scissors.

Figure 214: YES Store display of handmade toys. When I worked in the store, I sketched during slow times.

Figures 215-220: Displays or things for sale at the YES Store: handmade baskets, painted vests by Cow in the Kitchen Co., patchwork angels by Mary Durr, toy bear, hobbyhorse and handmade yarns turned into wearable art.

Figure 221: Mary Durr's sweet patchwork angel.

Figure 222: Scissors, rubber stamp design.

Figure 223: Basket, rubber stamp design.

Figure 224: Sweet heart.

Figure 225: Handmade baby dress by Hillary and Heather at the YES Store.

Figure 226: Border for advertisement for Small World.

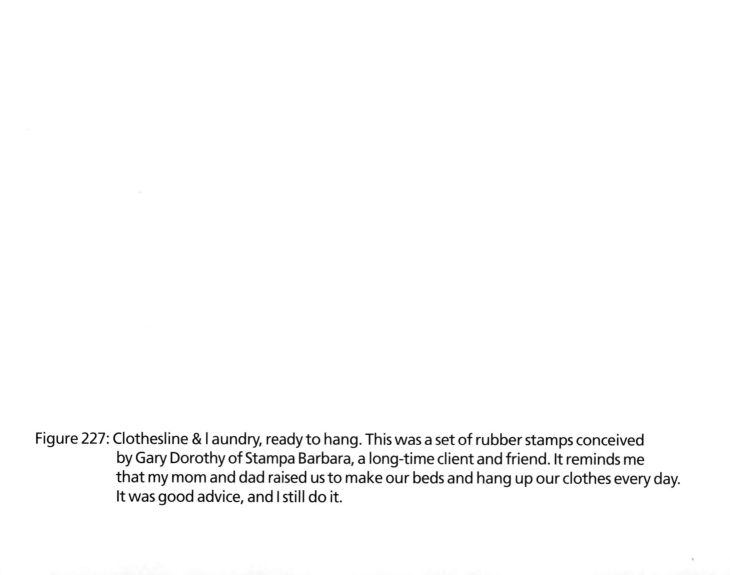

Figure 227: Clothesline & laundry, ready to hang. This was a set of rubber stamps conceived by Gary Dorothy of Stampa Barbara, a long-time client and friend. It reminds me that my mom and dad raised us to make our beds and hang up our clothes every day. It was good advice, and I still do it.

Figure 228: Letter-writing cats, design for stationery.

Acknowledgments

Thanks to my parents for giving me this life and the good fortune my dad said came from being Irish. They told me my talent came from my great grandmother Harriet. They put great emphasis on getting projects done correctly and on time, graduating from college and getting a credential, so that an artist could actually earn money! They allowed me the freedom (with a lot of guidance) to become myself, despite much eyebrow raising.

I would also especially like to thank my husband, Armin Müller, on whom I have depended as my counselor, supporter, and sound thinker. He's a smart and charming person. I have given him many opportunities to help me, and he has always followed through. He is my best friend and lasting love, and has worked small and large miracles on my behalf for twenty-five years. He's my hero. Our motto, like Noel Coward's, has been: "Work is more fun than fun." And we have accomplished great things while having a very good time of it. A wonderful life, intricately woven and connected, branching, but going forward in the same direction. Two branches, one tree. My flashes of inspiration, which seem so simple at first, have often involved his help. And he has never declined a request for his assistance. I have benefited in so many ways from knowing him. Thanks, Armin.

I also thank Tom Moore, my wonderful friend of twenty years and business partner (Inkling Rubber Stamp Company), whose intelligence, constant support, and ability to help put this book together (including scanning all but the oversize images) have been a delight to me. Plus, he's a really sweet guy!

Finally, thanks to John Daniel, Susan Daniel and Eric Larson of Fithian Press; to Paul and Doug at Photolith for scanning the largest drawings; to Bill Horton, Wayne McCall, and Tom Bradley and the staff at Graphic Traffic for their assistance in getting us proofs; to David Dahl, for his literary advice, ideas, and friendship; and to Tony Askew for his liner notes. And thanks to all the nice people who've asked me for my work over the years. This book is a testimony, not only to "work," but to lasting friendships most of all.